My Composite Self

Emerson McL. Daniel

Authored by Emerson McL. Daniel

Cover Design: Marcia M Publishing House

Cover Photography: Emerson McL. Daniel

Interior Design : Catherine Williams, Chapter One Book Production

Edited by Marcia M Publishing House Editorial Team

Published by Marcia M Spence
of Marcia M Publishing House
West Bromwich
West Midlands
UNITED KINGDOM B71 1J

ISBN: 978-1-913905-02-6

www.marciampublishing.com

Time is love
Love is time
Time is now
Now is love

In memory of Walter Charles Nelson
and Jean Elizabeth Nelson,
my parents and all that I am

The Queen of Spades came to see me
with all her suited royalties.
She soothed, why don't you take one of
my hearts to keep you company,
and you can have my clubs and my
diamonds to sing you a symphony…

Maybe

Maybe

she feels I'm not here at all

Maybe

she knows I don't give a damn

Maybe

she's thinking I'm sick of this romance

Maybe

she wants to know where she stands

Maybe

she's surmising that we are not going anywhere fast.

Beyond the valley
Her voice resounds
Like Echo and Narcissus
Only a pool
Reflects the gloom in her eyes
Showing something
That she can't have
But knowing truly
It is hers all along

Maybe

she's thinking of leaving my life

Maybe

she has realised I'm what Salinger called a phoney;

That I'm just a faker
A sweet-talking womaniser

On the wind
I catch a hint of Chanel No.5
In the corner of my eye, I see her
Tiptoeing by
Dressed in an expensively cut
Figure-hugging
Enticing
Easy to unzip
Versace 1920's styled dress
Her breasts tightly encased,
Still give the impression of escaping their provocative cage
Like maybe her feelings
That I'm not here at all
But in a time-vacuum
Beyond comprehension
And reasoning
Lost in the solace of her maybe's...

The Awakening

She talked all night,
About a reoccurring dream.
She talked all night
About someone called Gilman.

She said she feels awakened,
After reading Chopin and bell hooks.
She said she identifies with Simone de Beauvoir
And didn't want to be like the woman in the yellow wallpaper.

She said, you are a beautiful man
And I love you…
God, I do love you;
But what I want you can't give me
Where I want to go, you can't take me.

She effused I want to fly…
I want to see things through my own eyes;
I don't want to see them through yours.
I want to feel for real
The things I feel inside
I want to be true to me.

Gaia

Watching you
Watching you
Watching you ever-changing
Your colours of spring – translucent green now
Golden yellow when you come to another end.

Your kisses in April
Fall in sheets
Washing away winter's grey
Diluting my compressed mind…

Your coldness
Penetrates
All that lies deep
(All that cannot be seen)
Festers
Away from curious eyes
Away from diagnosis
Spreading like ripples
Seeking the sides of memory's lake.

I cannot forget your moods of anger,
As your storm clouds race rapidly
Across your brow
Your temper like Hephaestus' fire
Spewing out words
You seem not to regret – what do they mean?

But I loved you then
Perhaps more than before – How could I not?
For never were you more beautiful – resplendent
Striding across the earth, sea and sky in majestic guise

Knowing whatever you do could not be wrong
Feeling insignificant to your destructive wont
Praying in your blind unfairness, you'll pass me by

Watching you
Watching you
Watching you change to a slight draft
Gently whispering against my skin
Making me gulp as I catch my breath.

Looking for the King

Mr Man raged, "I've been hooked since I saw him aged nineteen
At the age of ten
And when he died...
I knew it couldn't be the end!"

He got on an aeroplane and flew over the western plain

Landed in Tennessee

Checked into a cheap motel
Stating 'I'm looking for the King.'

Mr Man wandered from town to town in a battered old tired Chevrolet
In an outback steakhouse, he stood looking for signs
His white flared suit dirty with grime
His dyed black hair blown out of place
And his tassels riding the warm hazy breath of a breeze.
He entered shouting, 'I've come looking for the King.'

Mr Man sat on a rock,
Looking across a lonely barren landscape
On Indian land that'd witnessed war dances and sacred rites
He finger-combed his hair from his face,
As he hummed...
"Keep offa my blue suede shoes... Love me tender, love me true..."

He climbed to a height
Answering the voice he thought he'd heard
Whispering, "When you smile the world is brighter...
Heartbreak is so lonely
Heartbreak is so lonely, baby..."
He howled, "Got my mojo working!" swinging his legs. Gyrating his hips
To the ghosts whose spirits sail the winds
Before launching himself into the desert air
Crying,
"I've found the King!"

Sweetness

Sweetness I love your pretty funky dress
And when you wear that smile, I love you the best.

Sweetness I've got to confess I'm going crazy since I saw you
I've been kinda keeping tabs on you – give me your address!

Sweetness gotta get you this letter – give me your phone number
I want to tell you that I need your sweet caress.

Sweetness I love your crazy expressions
Love the way you hold your head when you do your weird impressions...

Sweetness when you dance it begs romance
Let me show you tenderness.

Sweetness when you laugh as though you couldn't careless
I love you the best.

The Bugle Call

"My Mother," He murmured,
"Is pure evil…
Pure evil and true.
She epitomises what that bloke said,
'They fuck you up
They really do.'
Her words – her serpent tongue,
Bounds the natural curious soul; its innocence,
Constricts it – squeezes the life out of it.
Replaces it with fear
Reeling in an ocean
Of bewilderment, self-loathing, anger and hate.

A gasp of breath, in disbelief,
Is tightly crushed by the all-powerful snake
Coiled around life's flagging torso.

When the anomie of the mind is not enough,
The blows fall;
Pummelling the body,
As if motherless.
Propelling it from one corner to the next
Like a rag doll
In a dog's mouth
Like the dog she is…
Growling her mad imagined thoughts and insane jibes,
Emanating in seething rhetorical questions.
Her wild eyes bulging

To the point of bursting out
Of their furious sockets.

After she is spent
Tired, like someone who has laboured ...
Once her rage and manic state,
Abates - ebbing like the sea, leaving the shore it has pounded,
She conjures stories,
To make excuses for the marks...
To give lies for the flowing blood,
The broken bones - set to be deformed.
She mumbles, incoherently, soft words
That fall on the bruised petrified mind,
Lying crumpled and battered.
Wondering why nothing
Came of the bugle calls
Sounded again and again."

The Man Who Thought Himself A King

A long time ago, when life was quite short
There lived a man who thought himself a king
And treated everyone as though they were ruled by him
He didn't have a kingdom or a throne;
There wasn't one left to own or to steal
Only a relatively nice home.
One day someone said hello,
Out of courtesy, for it was a gorgeous day
But he thought they'd said, "Your Majesty."
To which he drew his sword – one that was made of wood
And painted brilliant silver with a grip in fool's gold
And bellowed, 'On your knees, sire
Let me bestow upon you the title of Sir Knight
And for your lady knight let her be now called Dame
Upon her let me claim my right for I'm King
Ordained by God Almighty to all on which you walk."
But the Dame recoiled, "No."
Though she was faintly flattered to be desired by the thought of royalty.
Realising there was nothing to be had
He stowed away on a ship, pulled by a thousand oars
For a land he was sure laid beyond the horizon calling
Where he would jump into the charmed sea and swim for shore.
So, he sailed for a hundred days and one more
Hidden and concealed
Surviving on stolen rations and salivation
Until one morning he was convinced he'd spied the pencil line of an island
With mirage trees protruding; waving and dancing as if for him in supplication
He leapt – a leap of faith

His virgin sword tightly clasped between his teeth his boots around his neck
Into an ocean teeming with kings and queens, princesses and princes
Who raced and flew in a surge of glory instantly cutting him in two
Recognising his kingship, they left his crown
Which bobbled to and fro expectant and proud,
Still with his sword clenched between his teeth in the crimson-gowned sea.

Go Tell the Spartans

And so I walk my spear in hand my shield on my shoulder
the battle has been fought
bloody and violent everywhere smoulders
no victor no loser just a sacrifice to the god Death

But again I will take my stand in the line
advancing to the sound of the pipe
to combat my foe who looks like me
and thinks like me

Didn't the poets say
to die bravely is glory
men will sing your name
and do you honour
thus gain immortality

But Oh ~ Oh my wife, my child
will I not see your faces again?
will I die far away on foreign soil?
my body stripped of its spoils
eaten by the vultures and rats
never again to be near you to feel your warmth

But I hear the noise the roar of war
I see you shackled my child put to the sword
so I must go to combat my foe
who looks like me and thinks like me
with your love within my breast
and the thoughts of the poets

To sacrifice my life
to die bravely
so that men will sing my name
and do me honour
so gain immortality

The Voice

Whilst I was sleeping,
Someone called my name
Woke me up from the dreamiest sleep I'd ever had.
The voice was rough without warmth or welcome
It had an urgency that spelt danger,
Unless its bidding was done immediately
I pretended I was deep in slumber –
In the land of make-belief.
However, the voice was incessant,
Calling and calling my name
Using different tones
Anger worked.
When I reluctantly opened my eyes, there standing before me
Was someone I'd thought I'd never see in my humble abode,
At this time.
He spluttered, "So you're awake at last are ya?
Had enough of pretending did ya?" and gave a hearty laugh
"Well, ya didn't expect to see the likes of me, did ya?"
He roared; tears tricking down his ghostly mask.

Wrong Side of Town

I was walking on the other side of town
When a man came up to me…
He hissed,
"What are you doing here, Boy
What are you doing on this side of town
Don't you know you don't belong?
By now, you should know you shouldn't be!

You people contaminate everywhere you go
You are like rats – worse than rats
You do nothing but breed
You're worse than any disease – a plague.

Get out of here, Boy
Before I beat you to your knees
Before I get your disease
We don't want your kind here
We want to stay pristine…

This time I'll let you go
Be pleased you came across me on my own
Thank your lucky stars the boys are all at home.
Go now that you know
That here you don't belong…

You should never – never be
You're a mistake
Worse than any disease
Can't you hear me?

I said go
Get out of here!
Thank your lucky stars you've come across me on my own
Don't come back…
Or we'll beat you to your knees!"

April 18th Five

I never thought today would come
All of those yesterdays
When we whiled the time away
When we climbed mountains
Waded through oceans
Cloaked the torment time can inflict

Do you remember running to a standstill?
Your face
Flushed with the effort of trying
Your hair windswept
Like a demented warrior
On a battlefield of insane valour

Didn't we love
Like Shiva? Like Ares and Aphrodite?
Didn't we sow seeds
Like Titans resting on our every word?

I never thought the mist would clear
To reveal that one course
I thought we'd navigated through
I thought we'd given a wide berth to.

If walls were recorders of time
Like old photographs, you see staring
From mildewed books; from old speckled films
What images they'd have stored
Of ups and downs
Of frustrated dreams.
Of bright, bright days
Of shattered you, broken in pieces
A demeanour of loss and confusion

And me wondering if the spoken word
Is truly more powerful than that written
Like those said
Before the third crowing of the cock.

Who would have guessed
That beyond the tender caress
That after the sacred dance
You and I would become like toys
Tossed around in the game of life
Leaves blowing in a swirling wind
Ships being battered on a stormy sea
The flickering flames
Unguarded from a child's innocent breath
Who would have guessed?
Who would have guessed?

If

If I steal the moon
Give you the earth
Pluck the stars from the sky
Empty the oceans
Crumbled the mountains into the finest sand
For you, all for you
Would that be enough for you?
Cause if it's not
What more could I give?
Only my skin and bones
My humbled knees
My prostrated hands.
If these are not enough
What more?
Steal Jupiter and Mars too
In a case of Venus
To give to you.
If you ask for the hours the minutes the seconds
Every pause of my hesitant breath
All for you… all!
A song?
Verses of Persian poets?
All the jewels in the world
Even those buried beneath the sands of the wine-dark sea
From the beginning of time
If all of these I give to you?

A Band of Bigots

They sit glued – fixated
Staring at the screens
Fingers splayed typing eyes searching
Their faces light up when they discover
The sound of an instrument
With an unusual name:
Djembe, hurdy-gurdy, balafon, ocarina

They want to share…
Are eager to share
The beautiful charm of the sitar
One cooed, it sounds like angels
Charming mankind to sleep

The funny thing is
They are relaxed consumed
Immersed in sounds of foreign instruments
They are discovering
Have no boundaries
Though made by alien hands
And formed by distant tongues.

Hege Mony

Are you God…?
You?
Deciding who should live and who should die…

Are you God…?
Taking what you want?
Destroying all…

Are you God?
Calling me what you want?
Telling me what to say…
Making me do what I don't want?

Are you God…?
You?
Are you God…?

Ballad (Oh Woman)

Oh, woman, I've got to leave you
I've got to leave you.
Your father says I'm not right – not right
He says I've come up on a down train,
He says I've fallen in a shower of rain – in a shower of rain.

But woman, if he could see what I feel inside for you -
What I feel inside for you.
If he could see the magic in our hearts
If he could see the beautiful butterflies that flutter in me
When you speak of us being one.

Oh, woman, I've got to leave you
I've got to go somewhere far; away from his keen blade –
Somewhere far... where you cannot reach me,
Where you cannot hear me cry – where you cannot hear me cry.
Your father says there is something not right with me
He says had I not been wrong
Had I not been wrong...

But woman if only he knew what I feel
When you hold me...
If only he could see what we are like
When we are together – when we are together!

Oh, woman, I've got to leave you –
I've got to leave you...

A Day

It was a day
When the day was melting…
There was a song playing on the radio,
'Hey, America, It's Christmas Time!'
It seemed funny that a cold song
Could make a day
But it's the way I guess.

I heard someone say, "It is going to be hotter
Tomorrow, hotter than today!"
My mind abandoned me and dived down below the sea.
A breeze like someone's breath blew
It was so hot the drinks fought to be perspired.

Someone asked,
"How about some food?"
Food for thought, I thought.
Overhead a plane flew high in the sky
Like a minute hand

I longed for an air-conditioned room,
A cold shower.
Couldn't be enticed
By the smell of beautiful perfume.

Aletheia

I didn't know what I was looking for
I'd searched and searched
Doing my best to avoid trouble and all of its friends
When I found myself in the middle of a damned field
I stood, palms shielding my eyes
Peering into those invisible lines
Connecting today tomorrow and yesterday
Wondering if I'd recognise her – if I saw her
Wondering if I'd know
Meteorites of diamonds plunged grazing my face
Stardust sparkled danced before my curious bloodshot eyes
If the east was the south
If west was north
I was wide awake
Wide awake

All In My Head

God made me I'm told
If you want to go
God loves me I'm his
If you want to go
God makes me cry
Ain't nothing I can do
God makes me feel pain
Ain't nothing I can do
God makes me see suffering
If you want me to lie
God pretends no prayer can be heard
If you want me to lie
God allows me to play with fire
If you want to cry
God teases me
If you want to cry
God the son the Holy Ghost
It ain't true
God have mercy on me cleanse my soul
It ain't true
I know a place
If you want to go
Without a name
If you want to go
No street no town
Ain't nothing I can do
In no country
Ain't nothing I can do

There are no invisible lines
If you want me to lie
No peacocks seducing humanity
If you want me to lie
No half for you ninety-nine and a half for me
It ain't true
There is no beginning no end
It ain't true
It is all in me – All in my head.

Anger

Anger is my closest friend
It sleeps inside me – choking me
Its heat burning me up inside.

Tastes like water on a parched tongue,
Like sugar in a bitter mouth,
Like love in an orgy.

Anger is my closest friend
My volcanic ally,
Following me where ever I go…

Makes me feel sorry for some of the things I've done
Makes me feel brave when I'm desperate.

Anger is my salvation
My redeemer
My drive – My burden
My closest friend

Anonymity

You conceal your gender
Your characteristics your emotions
In a chamber buried deep within the caverns of chance
Your essence resembles summer; fruit jam on freshly baked bread
Ground coffee with sugar to the heart's desire
Fluffy and warm
Against your supposed price of comfort
Ambition tastes bitter and vile.
Your refusal to remove your coat on sweltering days
Is spiteful – a merry dance with fickle fortune
You beg only one comparison
You are total like death.

Balthazar

I brought you gold,
As you laid sucking your fingers
Between squawking and wailing,
Searching for the teats from above…
I rocked you, smiling, to sleep
Humming a lullaby.
You weren't blue
Nor emerald
Nor were you hay or straw
When I laid you down to sleep
I prayed to you my soul to keep.
I was young then
Almost a child myself,
In the great scheme of things;
The day I travelled from afar
With the bearers of frankincense and myrrh
Full of hope and cheer
Forgetting man's propensity
To peg to the stake
Anyone with a glint of light in their eyes.
Now I'm old,
Bitter and disappointed
By hope's tricks and deceptions…
Faith has liquefied drowning the spirit
Like lead thrown into a river of lava.
These hundreds of years
Have been chains of iron –
The lash of the tongue

As I cling searching for the essence of my soul
My only song,
Sung once a year
When I'm called wise
Shown to be in splendid guise,
A contradiction to the rest of the year
Of invisibility and insignificance…
A perpetual crucifixion of denial
But – still, I rise from my comforting bed,
Despite my doubts;
Optimism and dented confidence
My guides stumbling through
A travesty of contradictions
As I traverse this shrouded land
Picking my way
Over paths promising nothing
Wishing for a gift of gold.

Billogmoomoo

You know, I think you're kind of special,
like one of those occasions that happens once every four years.
You know, I get up in the mornings listening to the radio
but the voices I hear are yours,
And the news is like a story being told of you...
My imagination replaces my reality with you.
You know I was sitting on a train – I can't remember where I was going – perhaps I was in my car...
Anyway, I sat watching the landscape going by, from rural to urban; from clear blue sky to smog...
And I thought, wouldn't it be nice if we could escape for a while, you know, on one of those shuttle rides so we would literally leave the world?
But I laughed to myself, as I thought,
I'm out of this world already.
You have sent me to somewhere I thought only existed in books and poems...
I wonder if this is the place where Mark Antony and Cleopatra visited before they died?
And Romeo and Juliet!
"Crazy, crazy you..."
I hear you say,
"You crazy mad fool!"
I don't care, as long as you say that silly thing... what is it?
"Billogmoomoo!"
I love it when you say that...
It makes your eyes sparkle...
Makes me want to boogie right there and then to some inaudible music.
You know those processions you see in Indian literature of Krishna or, I imagine, those Bacchanalian frenzies of intoxication and merriment?

It's like one of those...

It's like one of those.

I suppose it's like being kissed for the first time. You know, truly kissed,

Like that passion that makes you offer your breasts to be devoured...

To be touched like some sacred shrine.

When the winter comes, we'll catch snowflakes

To see if they really are all different...

And if you want, we'll fly away with a snowman,

And ask to be put down where the northern lights react to your aura,

The colours representing

The craziness I feel.

That would be good, wouldn't it?

It should keep a mad scientist busy for a while trying to figure that one out!

Anyway, you know, I 've got to go (I'm already gone - mad... mad as the Mad Hatter) - Billogmoomoo

To seek, to find...

To lose myself...

To lose myself...

To try and get to base...

Before I'm ticked.

Blacker than Black

Blacker than black the night cries
Throw in a thousand rainbows
Cast me to the winds
Swirling across the oceans and the sky
Upon me write a lullaby.

Autumn Day

The strings waver and quiver,
Sounding cello-like…
Groaning and moaning a weird happiness;
Like a broken heart.

On the hill conifers bend before commencing,
To strut their slim figures on a musical breeze,
Next to the leafless oaks standing in dread –
Not strong enough to hold on to their own.

Those lie abandoned… scattered. Strewn gold,
Blown on concrete paths and busy roads,
Crushed mercilessly under polluting wheels
As they seek the earth's entombing, patient mouth.

The steaming kettle whistles,
Emulating the 12:35 traversing fields; yielding willingly.
Its scolding steam mists the panes looking across
At the autumn sun hitting this side of the wall…
Reflecting like a holy thought,
On the still water of the flowing river;
Free of men reciting their rehearsed lines to pull a catch.

The radio talks about being in shock,
From the day's news.
Then immediately changes its tune,
To four four times and three four times
As if nothing had happened.

Boudicca

I met her on a mountain top,
Looking for awesome energy, she gushed.
These are so much more than mere stones and rocks, she rasped,
Pointing to the mountain's face.
Up here the earth is poetic, on the ground; it has an awesome energy,
Here it is awesome...
It makes me tremendously, deliriously giddy.
I don't suppose you can guess where I've just flown in from can you?
I'll give you a clue
It's a fruit...
So good they named it twice?
It's a tiptop place
Especially getting starry-eyed knocking down Godfathers
Whilst killing time in Dublin in Manhattan.
I didn't ring a soul whilst I was there,
Though it's so much better than writing; it's such a marathon
And I do love a chinwag...
It was an epic adventure
Epic... I loved it. I had such a smashing time
Walking and exploring – being the flaneur
It's terribly wonderful being able to talk to you
To someone free
Free so I can re-enact everything without pausing for breath...
I belong in the court of Kings.
I'm Briton before the self-appointed... antebellum
Just in case you hadn't guessed!
Didn't you know?
Queen and country and all that, she cooed,

Like sweetness and light
Then she sang la de da…
La de da; similar to Julie London crying a river.
Wouldn't it be marvellous to have…?
To have some of the sun from Spain
When it rains on their plain?
Wouldn't it be marvellous for them to have
Some of what we have all of the time?
Darling, just think how divine that would be
Imagine it…
A healthy glow!
You do know what I mean?
Don't you, darling?
Oh, you do!
Suddenly, she announced,
Today is my birthday
It's the pinnacle of my life
My watershed moment…
Then threw herself off a crag like an eagle
I watched her fall… falling.
Her tawny hair soaring up to me – burnt gold,
As an inverted waterfall might
Then glided, unlike Icarus.

Conqueror

What would you say, conqueror...?
Has your Homer succeeded,
In voicing your success and illumination
Exhorting your praise
Interpreted today by mere souls
In mere words?

You've become water,
In all its different forms;
Some swill you away,
In their search for gold.
Some quench their thirst
Like thirsty children,
Whilst some drink with sugar or salt
Fruit or alcohol ... all swayed
By nearly three millennia
Of microbrewing...

We; judge, jury, executioner
Perched on our antique thrones
Like to think,
We are better...
Better examples; better role models.
Sinless with washed hands
Superior – godlike
What do you think, Conqueror?

Covering Science

Today
What a day!
A thousand manic voices rang like a bell
In a pollution of impolite noises and insults.
To make matters worse,
The harsh hours dragged slowly
Crawling at the pace of a snail,
As if they wanted each second to take its toll…
To leave their mark on my frazzled mind.

A voice asked – begged…
Wanted to know if my no could be a yes,
When I grunted and shook my head to a toilet request
Whilst another called me mean,
And said it was against their basic human rights.

There was a time for a moment's respite;
A time for a cup of tea
And yesterday's prepared snack that looked the way I felt.
A time to catch my breath and sigh
But this wasn't to be…

Time was being made up for being lost and late,
For being wasted
For being disruptive.
Defiant faces became contrite
Knowing they'd missed a break in their mundane day.

The afternoon moved on heavy legs... a lumbering gait
Against an echo of resentful breaths exhaling
Knowing silence must be maintained.
My mood lightened, with the thought of the end...
With the image of a piled steaming plate
Full of the fragrances of the distant east and the deep ocean.

Death on the Nile

Death on the Nile
At half-past nine – Sunday;
Eating cucumber sandwiches
Battenberg cake, scones with jam and cream.

Between easy chat,
Meandering strains of Elgar resonate
And recital of Keats;
Interrupted with debates on Darwin
Floating to and fro
Mingle with easy laughter.

What you do to me… Do you know?

Do you know what you do to me…?
Do you know how you make me feel…?
Do you see the sparkle in my eyes when you smile…?
Do you know the ache I feel inside…?
Do you… Do you… Do you…?

Eve to Judgement Day

Looking out of the window at the falling rain
my breath misting the pane

Lovers walking down the road oblivious
laughing – I bet – at the most trivial of jokes

Children playing in puddles
paying no attention as their mothers scold

A monochromic grey-like covering
occupies the sky and my mind

The window reflects the loss in my eyes
and runs like the tears I've cried

The inevitability of it gnaws at my flesh like maggots
all words devoid of emotion

Sound only hollow and empty
just syllables and consonants falling to the floor

Shattering, sizzling like cold water in a hot frying pan

But looking out of the window at the pouring rain
each drop falling like the burden of inevitability and certainty

I've seen the names written on the wall
I've seen the pain in frightened eyes

And as the days come around, I've seen the dread
no composure can disguise

Don't ask me to lend a hand
I'm so weak I can hardly stand

My body like the pavement and the road becoming wet
the trickle of sweat perspiring from my head

From under my arm running down my back
each drop mocking

How can I forget the emptiness I've created?
How can I ask forgiveness for my moment of madness?

First and Last Goodbye

Do you remember that summer?
I think it was the hottest on record!
We walked across sun-scorched fields,
Singing at the top of our voices to Maggie May,
As it played on your cream transistor radio.

You said you'd always remember this day – this Saturday
In agreement, I nodded, lost in thought –
My mind caught up in our game of pretend swordplay
And knocking the heads off the tall dried grass.

It wasn't long after,
When you were struck by the dart piercing your heart;
Innocence died then – leaving
Floating to a place where youth resides.

I knew things would never be the same,
When I saw the smile in both your eyes
And you both vowed till death to part.
I knew I'd never see you again...
I knew you were going away; you always said you would
I knew you were travelling along a road only wide enough for two.

It was a cold, miserable day when you took to the sky
When we hugged and said our first and last goodbye,
I could feel your happiness in your urgent embrace.
I wanted to say,
You could write telling me your secrets

Like once you did…
When we ran free and wild
When we howled with laughter
Unable to stand, as if nothing else existed
In our world, where the sun would never set.

Gold

I'm the biggest number I know
Bigger than always
Smaller than forever.
I'm an odd one
Though I'm perfect –
A perfect even number…
I'm gold; Mansa!
A golden age
Unlike silver and bronze;
Always less and lesser
Poor second and third.

Guppy

She gently glides to the bottom of the murmuring glass depth,
Her billowing wings elegantly fanning the murky water
In swirls of geometric patterns
Turning her scales a dull, tired gold.
I think she's had a belly full of being trapped - contained
Captured to be stared at…
To adorn this empty full room, for the study of science
For the love of someone who abandons her
Throughout the day and night,
Except for a blind admiring glance when he drops his morsels of confetti feed
Sprinkled from his Godlike hand; autumn leaves
Into a world, a lifetime of his study wouldn't educate him to understand.

She's a long way from home,
Further than her audience travel
Each day even if multiplied by a hundred scores.
Her large curious eyes are big and round like mine
They follow me when I go to take a closer look…
When I move above her tank, she comes to the top
To look me straight in my face
As if pleading, like a child wanting to be picked up…
To be loved. To be allowed to run free

I feel deep sympathy for her
In her small lonely algae edged cage,
Gurgling away electrically
Day after day. Alive.
Dimming the light in her sad sparkling eyes.

Hey Pauline

"Hey Pauline, where are you going? Why have you got that book in your hand?
I was just about to call for you, to ask you if you want to go for a walk down to the park or something...
Do you fancy it? Do you...?
Do you want to rollerblade? Hey... hey Pauline, do you fancy going to the park with me?
I saw Mrs Innocents, our PE teacher, the other day and you'll never guess who she was with...? Actually, snogging him right out in the open!
Isn't she married?
I saw her with a man once; I thought he was her husband. He was a right dish as well, the kind of bloke who looks like a popstar.
Hey Pauline, if you want, we can go to the pictures... your mum won't mind, will she?
I think your mum is cool, she lets you call her by her first name...
I tried that with my mum, and she almost knocked my head off.
She said, "Listen..." She said, "Who do you think you are addressing young lady? Off to your room now and learn some respect."
It's not as if I'm that young either.
Hey Pauline, are you and Taylor doing it? Are you?
Go on tell me, I promise I won't tell anyone not even Alistair...
Go on tell us, and I'll tell you if I have... Go on!

I was going through my mum's wardrobe the other day...
You'd never guess what I found!
I can't believe my mum and dad could do anything like that.
They're disgusting... at their age as well you'd think they'd know better.
Hey Pauline, I hate that cow Diane Freya she is such a bitch.
All the guys fancy her just because she's got big uns.
Everybody thinks she's clever, but I am cleverer than her, and you are...

We are in a higher group than she is!
She thinks she is something special just because she goes out with all the boys who have left school, the cow her.
Hey Pauline, did you see what's his name on the TV last night? Oooooh wow, He Is So COOOL, so DISHY! I've got his posters all over my bedroom even on the ceiling.
My dad's always telling me to take them down. He is such a pain. Moan, moan, moan, "In my day this, in my day that." He's like a dinosaur!
Hey Pauline, has your dad bought you that new thing yet? Your dad is great. He never tells you off, and he looks at me real nice.
He's always pleased to see me. I can tell he likes me... doesn't he? Hey Pauline? He likes me...!
I bet you're jealous, aren't you? Aye... Aye? I bet you are!
Hey slow down, what's the matter with you anyway? Why are you carrying that book?
Is it from your grandma?
My grandma bought me one once, but my dad threw it away and said it was a load of crap.
My mum said, "If it was from your mother you would not have done that."
Guess what he said then...?
He said, "you are like your mother, full of crap."
And then he gave me a cuddle and pinched her bum.
He is a funny bugger, my dad; I don't know what my mum sees in him sometimes.
Hey Pauline, can I come with you? Can I?
Where are you going anyway? Hey Pauline?
Where are you going?
Hey Pauline, what's up?"

I Love You

I love you,
More than the tenderness
Breaking me in two,
More than when I am inside of you…
I love you.

When I feel less than I think I could ever be,
My aching bones, my thumping heart,
Will always come to you to quench my thirsty soul.

I love you as if there were
No yesterday, no tomorrow.
No anything that can ever be.
No anything that has gone before.
I love you.

I'm Your St Christopher

I'm your St Christopher,
Your cunt on the side.
Give it to me
Hard and true
Under a bridge,
On a cool summer's night,
Against a sharp jagged wall.

Come the call...
Come when you really want it...
Come when you need me.

I'm your horse...
Your rocking horse,
Wooden and rigid – unbreakable,
A broad back to take the whip
A pompous flank for your spur...
A hair-covered bod
To hide the bruises.

Come the dressage...
Come the hunt... the call
Come when you need me.

Jane

She was only Sixteen
From the sunshine state;
A weak-looking thing, freckled
With pale blue eyes; cold and calculating.
She shot it, while it grazed – a behemoth
With one single shot
More powerful than her innocent frame
She took its hide and its proud head…
Then the ants came, like flies
With their choppers and axes to carry the carcass
On their strong backs,
In their bloodied arms and mandibles;
Their price for their hungry blind conspiracy.
She laughed – smiled for the man with the eye,
Like she'd smiled earlier
With her right booted foot resting on the still, warm beast
The smeared blood, on her cheeks,
An antithesis to the steel in her pale blue eyes.

July 28th 1989 – Grace's Thirty-Ninth Birthday

It was slowly approaching two, we were being silly; playing games and guessing what was true, whilst we finished the last of her compote, cheese and fancy biscuits and took a final mouthful of a red wine that tasted like vinegar.

"Christ!" she uttered, wine coming down her nose, like blood, staining her white blouse above her heart. She said she didn't know what day it was – she couldn't remember what day it was but was glad I was there with her, her one true love, who had stood with her, by her and had given more support than anyone she'd known. For a moment, I laughed… not one of those laughs when something makes a person have hysterics. But I laughed an ironic laugh; a kind of shy laugh which made her laugh too.

Looking at her eyes, I saw she was serious about not remembering what day it was. My stomach lurched as I hesitantly asked, "But you do know it's your birthday, don't you?" At that, she stared at me as if contemplating something far away then softly murmured, "Do you remember when we were young…? Girls really not knowing what was what! And the things our parents used to tell us and do… our mothers most of all. They were cruel! Weren't they cruel? The things they'd say to us?

They didn't protect us from the things they'd had to endure, did they? Didn't they fuck us up?
They should have saved us!
They should have made us feel loved.
I remember once my mum slapped me hard because my father had said I was smart for passing him his slippers. Another time she laughed and scoffed when I told her I wanted to go to university. I used to wish they'd just… di… disappear. Just…!

That time I was on the corner of our street, after we'd been to the school disco, saying goodnight to Stevie what's his name and having a laugh… she appeared from nowhere grabbed me by the back of the neck and started marching me home all the while hitting me… shouting at me… calling me dreadful things; asking and then telling me what happens to girls who behave like me and if that wasn't humiliating enough as soon as I was in the house I had to remove my underwear in front of her so she could inspect them… she kept on slapping me every time I cried, 'why?'

They made me feel so bad about myself…so messed up and scared. Him with his drinking, sexist, bigoted, womanising ways… she…! She was vicious and delighted in 'taking me down a peg or two.' It made me determined. Bloody determined to escape… I held onto anything I thought would save me! Worked my arse off at school… When it came to it, I made sure I chose a university as far away as possible from the pair of them… You'd think after all this time those memories would have faded, wouldn't you? They haunt me…haunt my dreams… suffocate me. Sometimes I find myself welling up and hear myself still asking, 'why?'

Later we walked over the fields where she lived – it was one of those smiling days in late July. She spoke incessantly about incidents from when we were kids that she could not forgive. I was due to move in two days' time, not far from where we'd come out, so wanted her to see the house to kind of cheer her up. However, she refused. Becoming annoyed when I insisted. She said she'd never see it. We walked silently for a while.

"You know what, Emma?" she eventually half-whispered almost half announced, "When I go I want to be as I'm now; the same head, the same voice, the same mind, the same body, the same everything." I didn't know what to say, apart from an inane selfish comment, but it deeply saddened me to hear her talk like that. It made me frightened. Very frightened and weak. Nothing I said or did made a difference, it was as if she was in a trance and needed to disgorge the well of pain inside of her. Early this morning, when the phone rang, I knew it concerned her; my gut feeling was it's something terrible, but I didn't guess, for a moment, it would be to say Grace had died during the night. She'd had a violent haemorrhage in her brain.

June 24th 2016 – Friday

Something lurks beneath the pond
With teeth of razor blades and claws of hate
It no longer darts away when approached…
Doesn't squirm or shy to the deepest depth
It is confident its nose will survive the air;
Its tongue will find others to lap the milk of the
Devil's kindness.
Something most thought had gone away
Did not destroy its boat after it had sailed.

Like a Rainbow

She loves,
With the force of nature;
A tsunami caressing my soul
Flooding my emotions;
A storm raging passion
Devouring my body,
Entwining our embrace as we climb.
Her tears are crystals falling…
Glistening on her cheeks;
Reflecting the light in her eyes
Like a rainbow.

Without You

Leafless trees
Stand
Beneath a gloomy grey heaven
Their leaves
Long scattered

Willows aching
Reaching down to the ground
Weep
Like Demeter
Lamenting her Persephone

The undulating hills
Promise
Hidden surprises
The visiting redwings
Weave through the despondent day
Veiling its cheery face

Spitting rain
Like mischievous children
Mock
Each drop
A blow
Like the thrust of a spear
Reinforced by the fierce piercing wind
Howling
Invisible

Love

Love
is like
blood in the snow
not a rose
not a gift bestowed
just cold.
Its kiss
is of a corpse
that stings my lips
not like
a hungry wish
but a stumbling secret
that should be told.

Love's words
lack sense
they are
devoid of reason
like bone dried leaves;
they are thoughtless
and cruel.
They bring a flow
of uncontrollable tears
rendering my body
weak torn prostrated
and writhing
on my hall floor.

On the Train to Manchester

On Saturday I caught the 09:11 to Manchester, to meet a woman for a drink and a bite to eat. For most of the journey, I thought about Eccles cake, Chelsea buns, macaroon slices and tarts from Bakewell, swigged down with tea from Singapore – white even without milk.

It had snowed during the night painting the hills pure and innocent crisscrossed by many washed black lines drawn in stones. On top of the Moors, the highest peak touched the lowest cloud threatening more snow or rain since it always seemed to rain in that part of the world.

At least the snow would know its true form when it made its way, in spates, down steep glades and rocky streams giggling, as its water slapped and tickled the tired bones.

Going at sixty miles per hour on a train isn't that fast – the scenery flashing past looked hurried because the windows were small… up close it revealed all as if sitting in a cinema on a Saturday afternoon, like I did when I was small, and the film started… pulling me into the screen instead of looking at a rectangular blank wall staring back at me.

It was peculiar thinking of meeting someone I didn't know. I wondered what she'd look like; her size and figure, the sound of her voice, her accent and carriage. I hoped she'd wear a dress despite it being cold. I hoped I'd like her. Desire!

I pondered whether she'd look like the picture she'd sent me; claiming it was recently taken though she looked years younger than the age she'd claimed to be. Most curious, how would she look when she ate and drank?

One of my friends told me he was crazy about eating habits and hated anyone seeing him when he ate. He thought it would turn someone off, if they saw him eating.

I caught the bug, not about myself but others. I couldn't stop staring at people when they consumed food. I'd become a child again – a parent to the child in me – hearing myself saying, "Don't stare, it's rude!"

Almost at Piccadilly, twelve minutes out, my stomach started to lurch churning my inside into a frenzy. It was as if I had popcorn in my sweltering gut, popping and exploding. I half expected to actually see something physical fly out of my ears or my nose. Counting one to ten was no good. Anything more was equally futile, as I couldn't stop studying my watch and the train kept on repeating, "Nearly there."

Patriotic Spring

A Patriotic Spring
Rages in a stream of forgetfulness and spite
Cursing around the barricade
Rooms, gardens and architecture bedecked by the exotic
Aligned fragments of the earth's core, not of these shores
Not so much taken as spoils of war
But, deceptions, tricks of the tongue, sticky fingers;
Profound greed and exploitation.
Distorted past deeply hidden by the shroud of time
Sings as if true
Pens replace swords
Sharper at a stroke than a stab or a slash
Social media's garnished pagan superstitions
Roll like tumbleweed through remote towns and empty minds
About the many stained by a few
More lies and persecutions strutting in a dance frenzy
Apotheosis to deny all that is right
All that is true and good
All that has come to pass, after the toil,
The tears of the years fell in an unprecedented foul swoop.

Prometheus Bound

"I don't know where I have been
but it is not here - nowhere near

Over the oceans and far away
where sea lions sleep and sea horses roam

Men scream and shout
not in anger, not in pain

Not from laughter, nothing remotely the same
their distorted faces know not why!

The earth turns and the gods sleep
Heaven is becoming hell

And men are becoming gods.

Pegasus spread your wings…
take me up, higher
than the heavenly sky

The stars are icicles suspended in time
like my dreams, they'll melt and vaporise.

O Father, O Mother I have come from
over yonder, way beyond beyond

I have seen the Pillars of Hercules
I have visited Tartarus

I have seen the earth as a fungus
growing bigger and bigger

The gods are asleep they will not stir
but in their dreams, they see chaos

And from chaos, they'll come!"

Puritan

He loves his genealogy
His wallchart chronicling his distorted history.
He wears his badge big, proud, loud
Tonight, a mask.

Lips of love on the crucifix
He'll burn on a hill - later,
When the sun rests,
With God on his side
Beside an intricate noose.

His arms gloved in red - drip
The children's - of the wind and sky,
The people of diamond, ivory and gold.

The Crossing Lady

She waddles hunched shouldered
Heavy footed, shuffling like an emperor
To the middle of the road;
Her stern pole held an arm's length
Away from her breasts, almost bursting through their restraint
Her luminous coat a bright summer plumage
Over her winter down feathers
Big like her smile
Bigger than her rotund four eleven frame.
She looks as if she'd break into a dance,
Given the chance to keep warm,
If music was played spontaneously,
As sometimes happens in movies,
Should someone take the place of the stick
Controlling the impatient revs of the engines
Hastening tomorrow's small, steady steps.
She waves a thank you not really seeing who she is waving to
Wanders back to her perch at the side of the road
Rosy-cheeked and misty breath
Vaporising in the air,
Periscopic eyes surveying - meerkat poised,
Voice cooing, "Hold on Love!"
As she starts to begin, again.

The Drover and the Herder

This is a story…
A story of love and glory
Between two people;
One a drover
The other a cattle herder
Who lived in a place where the land was harsh, the rivers ran dry
And the rocks glowed red under the scorching sun.

She became a he,
For the sake of being
She shaved her hair –
Cropped it neatly behind her ears,
Thinking it made her lie more true.

He was he and knew it
He could do and be whatever he wanted
But not a she – that was taboo.
He made all he surveyed his own,
Though not the she who had become a he
He wanted her to give herself freely
They were like the keys on a piano,
Except the B and the E

His heart missed a beat,
When one day the wind blowing against her shirt
Revealed what she thought she had concealed;
And her legs straddling the saddle
Showed more shapely than any man's.

She thought him fair
He thought her beautiful…
Her back gracefully arching, like the branches of the foxtail palm.

One lonely night,
Their feet ventured to sate
The hunger ravishing every sinew of their souls…
Their fingers entwined
They danced, moaning like the softness of the herd's;
Every night their fingers entwined
Their bodies writhed,
In the glory of their dance
To the music that knew no bounds –
No social norms, no cruel rules; no De-Humanising Acts
They danced like the wind between the clouds.

The Greatest Sight is of You in Sleep

The greatest sight is of you in sleep,
On satin sheets
Cover free;
Shrouded in your pale porcelain blue nightdress
With its dark blue Indian ink oriental vine pattern
Delicately thin – as gossamer –
Clinging to your contours and crevices
Exaggerating your curves, like gossip tells a tale
Lying face down
Your softly beating heart raising you buoyantly,
Like the sea's gentle rising swell
One arm outstretched, relaxed, carefree
The other folded under your face
Holding you tenderly
Afraid you might break.
Your posterior – forbidden fruit –
Protrudes, gestures, mocks resistance
Tempts temptation
Conceals a kingdom's downfall
Conceals resurrection, forgiveness, forgetfulness;
Conceals once upon a time...
Your legs stretched
Smooth, shapely and toned
Inert
Mask your yearning, desperation and rhythm
When we dance...

The Snake the Viper and the Serpent

The snake, the viper and the serpent, all invited me to tea
Their words coiled around my throat
Hissed,
"You're it; you've got to make a run for it
See how long it takes to find you...!"
See which one of us is going to have you.

The Supply

No one sees him
Words are kept in dried up mouths.
Should they come,
They are hesitant, forced, shy to be expressed...
They refuse to be pronounced
Their vowels and consonants become tied up and twisted
As if on foreign tongues.

The body seeks the furthest corner
Where it sits huddled up and concealed,
Like a long-forgotten book
Quickly overlooked covered in dust.

Roving eyes search for a smile – the twinkle of an eye
The forming of the mouth to say, "Hello!"
In the midst of the hustle and bustle,
Bodies – as if by the same pole
Adroitly avoid each other.

Whilst stares conveniently averted
Suddenly take an interest in ancient posters,
Manicured fingernails and polished shoes.
And open questions are elegantly batted
By deftly swung closed bats.

To Mary Mae

A beautiful “Hello,” to you.
Well here I am
Over seas and mountains
Across deserts, forests
Snow-covered lands
Under a burning sky

When I stop to think
I hear the breeze
Softly caressing
The reeds by the stream
Their voices
Whisper unlike anything I’ve heard before
Dry and weightless
Like a lullaby
Swaying my mind
Undulating my thought

The heat of the day
Makes a show of perspiration
Across the top of my lip
And clear beads decorate my hairline
Like jewels – pure and true
Sparkling in the sun
Yesterday, I went for a walk
For what seemed an age
Though in truth it was only a couple of hours
To a place of natural beauty

Sand – stormed shaped
The figures and contours
Were so awe-inspiring
I found tears flowing from my eyes.

I thought of you
So far away
So distant.
As I gazed
I discovered myself wondering
How storms could create
Such wonder
Such lost for words…
Such violence, such power
Rocks millions of years old blown away
Turned into God's sculptures
Then I thought it a slow destruction
Unlike our storm.

Mary Mae
Alone
Here
The earth moves
It moans
It creaks
And through this valley of death and amazement
It sings
Serenading the coldest of heart
Making a person fall in love with it
Making a person feel an urgent passion

Voices from long ago
Rise and subside
On Aeolus' gift
I feel I know them
Part of me belongs to them
Wants to lie in their hammock of recognition

If only you were here to capture the thousand different colours
All of one hue
If only you were here to see the insignificance
Of all we greedily gather and store for our winter...
I now realise
My place in the order of things
This landscape has witnessed beginnings, failures, successes, ends
It holds secrets
It smiles
And laughs when one listens
Mary Mae, it runs
Sprints...
Like a ballet dancer
It pirouettes and becomes airborne
It takes my breath away
Leaving a burning pleasure
Pounding against the cavity of my chest

All of those things you said
All of those things you cried
The tenderness in your eyes
Are here...

Uncle, Thomas

"You know…
I…
Look at you.
I see
You are me…
Are like me.
But here…
The things you say,
The way
You behave,
The ways you think
I should be,
Are contrary – insulting
To what you say
When you are…
Given the time,
When you are surveyed.
Are against…
Me."

VC

He lives in a run-down terraced house with water coming through the roof every time it rains.
Outside the gutter hangs broken, with ferns growing over the top of blistered rusted metal.

Michael Dayart is woken from his drink induced sleep, by the voices of a man and woman arguing about money in the street.
He crawls to the window to see the woman dressed in a short tight lycra skirt and a revealing top, asking the man to be nice to her.

In the background, people trundle along and cars amble by. A good throw from his gazing bloodshot eyes, in the nearby play area, children run around playing; a small group of mainly boys stand cheering and jeering some kids younger than them, smoking swearing, indifferent to who's there.

It's going to be Christmas soon, Michael Dayart thinks, as a bus passes with Christmas advertisements on its sides.
And as if reminded, he remembers that it is cold and crawls back to bed.

He scans the wretched room and looks at the crumbling plaster and the mildewed paper. He tries not to think. He doesn't want to think. It hurts him to think.
In the corner, beneath the free newspapers and old magazines, lies the VC, last night's take-away on top with all the other nights decaying like his yesterdays, his today and his tomorrow.'

There is a sudden rapid series of thumps on the door, and he lays still; cringing... forgetting that a good push will open it.

The landlord shakes him, asking him for the rent with each movement of his unsympathetic hand, but Michael Dayart pretends to be asleep.
The landlord punches him hard in the side, making him groan, making him cry.
"If you don't pay by tomorrow you can get out, this room is disgusting. Get it cleaned!
In fact, if you don't clean it right now, you can get out. Do you hear?" he screams in Michael Dayart's ear. "If it's not done this minute you can get out!" He shouts as he slams the door shut. "I'll be back in a minute!" He yells through the wall. "You better have it done, I'll be coming back in a minute, you scum. Make sure you do it. You hear?"

"Why me?" he whimpers. "Why me? Of all of them, why leave me alone? Why leave me behind?" Michael Dayart sobs as he buries his face in his tear-soaked pillow, his only companion. His only comfort.

Michael Dayart hears 'NO', said a thousand times, reverberating echoing around his weary mushed up mind; the mouths slowly forming the word. Spoken without spite. As a matter of fact. The accompanying smile devoid of warmth, ignorant of understanding saying, "Don't come back – move on!"

Then the loud, mad, chaos. The flashbacks.

Michael Dayart sees him fall. Michael Dayart sees them all fall slipping through his strong fingers dying in his arms. The screams. The screaming; some calling for parents, far away oblivious of the killing zones where hell reigns. Their only connections came in letters and packages from home, with best wishes; always sealed with love, take care; keep your head down, looking forward to having you back here with us!

Michael Dayart reaches for his works and pumps happiness into his veins and oblivion into his mind.

Michael Dayart lies upon his rotting bed; cold as the coming winter.

Michael Dayart, the preacher intoned, "has gone to heaven and will reside in the House of God."

Virginia Summerseat

Virginia Summerseat lives in the Riverside Manor, not far from the old railway lines that are only used for visiting steam trains, and all sorts of men with tripods and cameras and cheerful hellos, when she gallops her horse. She shares her many roomed house with five fat furry pedigree cats, named after feminist writers, and agitators from the twentieth century, as well as Hilda and Stephaney, her helpers to keep the dust down and the rooms freshly aired.

Virginia loves to order – well persuade – her gardener to follow her instructions, especially those to make her carrots worm proof and her aubergines more royal than the queen's.

She hates Thursdays. She hates Mondays, Tuesdays and Wednesdays too because they are not strong days; she only likes the weekends. Those were the best days of the week. Days that allowed her to do the things most people do in the week, as well as to sigh and laugh, clap and sing and say, "Bloody marvellous!" She loves her homemade bread and jam and when she feasts, her legs tremor beating a rhythm that sounds like a distant stampede, whilst she hums the tune to 'Favourite Things.'

Virginia speaks eloquently like Alice in Wonderland… perhaps more like the Queen of Hearts when she says, "Off with their heads!" When she gets very tipsy, with her friends who live in the big houses on top of the hill behind the trees blocking the long rows of terraced houses at the bottom, she becomes like marshmallow crying, "I'm not horsey… I'm not! I never wanted to be, but mamma and papa insisted and wouldn't have it any other way. When one's a child, one has no choice in the choices that are made for one."

She speaks in long sentences when she describes what she has seen and short plosive phrases to convey her excitement. She claims to despise vulgarity but shakes with mirth about the time she got a prick in her hand and put it in cider.

War

Oh God, Oh God!
It draws near… it draws near.
Dancing a jig over fields of tall, slender grass,
Cutting through ancient oaks in ancient forests
Across dry powdered desert sands.

I hear its bugle and its drums.
I hear its manic laughter,
I see its polished steel
Glistening in the sorry sun.

It trails black on the horizon,
Like a cloak draped on the day.
Its roar booming,
It's engine spitting.
I feel the quaking earth,
Trembling like me.

It's here…
Like all, I didn't think it could be,
Like all, I dread to see.
It is here.
It's here!
War.

We Were All Beautiful

We were all beautiful
When we were young
Weren't we?
Full of life's best
Even in ill-fitting clothes;
Jeans too big
Or too small tight - bought.
Singing songs out of tune
That would be excused,
Laughed at and dismissed
As foolish and charmed.

From My Window

Out of the window, far away
close to the crumbling wall
grows a plant. Its leaves are
lemon-yellow and lime-green colour;
its flowers look like small balls of shredded
paper of the brightest saffron-yellow.

Beyond the crumbling wall, a solid foundation
with a patio facing up to the sky, hidden by rain clouds,
a faint smell of yesterday's barbecue drifts...

In the house, built long ago – when Victoria reigned
live home-making people, with their 'how do you do?
Hello's and unsure, shy smiles.

The roof, glistening wet from the falling rain,
lies like an unmovable sheet awaiting a painter's brush...
an erect sentinel, its head lowered for times gone.

Across the field, over an old Roman road, runs the railroad carrying its loads
to places I'll never go to, places I've visited once or twice. Places I have no
desire to ever go to again. Places of curiosity. The movements of the trains
rumble, shaking the ground vibrating one's feet.

High on a hill the water towers, overlooking me...
Observes all that moves. Even the tiniest creature cannot go unseen,
so powerful are the eyes only an imagination can see.

On the crumbling wall, on the flowering plant, on the sky-gazing patio
and the home-maker's house – the rain falls relentlessly, sometimes gently,
sometimes hard.

As I stare from my window even though I know why
I can't help but ask, why?

Winter

Winter draws near
With its protracted claws
Its omnipotent spite

If it could feel the pain it inflicts
On weak skin
Old joints

If it could feel its inflexible mood
Its lack of compassion
Its oppression

If it could feel

Wish You Wouldn't Go

Winter sky brings snow...
In my heart I know you are going to go
I wish you wouldn't go
I wish you wouldn't go
Say you won't go

We got a little crazy
We said a few stupid words
But you know I didn't mean them
You know I was feeling low

Winter sky brings snow
Like a migrant bird
I know you are going to go
I wish you wouldn't go
I wish you wouldn't go
Say you won't go

When darkness falls
Like a curtain at the end of a show
And the light of the day ends
I know you feel it's time to go
I wish you wouldn't go
I wish you wouldn't go
Say you won't go

Winter sky is heavy with snow
To blanket the earth to blanket my mind
Like all things that grow
I know you are going to go
I wish you wouldn't go
I wish you wouldn't go
Say you won't go.

Zephyrus

You'd better hope there's no God...
You'd better pray there's no God
For no god would forgive you for what you're doing.
It doesn't matter how much incense you burn...
It doesn't matter how many temples you build
For no god would forgive you for what you've done.
You're wasting your time saying, "Praise be to him;
The Father, The Son, The Holy Ghost!"
No lament will cleanse your cold, cruel soul.

Paradigm Shift

Blue is the Delta
Blue is the blood in my vein
Blue, blue the thoughts going around my mind.

Blue are the notes
Blue are my strings
Blue, blue are the songs my heart sings.

Blue is the prism contorting the light shining on me
Blue is the place in the sky
Blue, blue is the ocean's spiritual stone.

Blue is my desire, my hope, joy and happiness
Blue are the red lights, the ambers and the green ones too
Blue, blue – the quintessence.

A Hero

A hero
To hoist the flag of revolution;
Revolution of common sense.

A hero to banish the opportunists' jibes
At all that is decent.

A hero that recognises those who toil
And those who want to toil
This sweet land's stubborn soil.

Emerald

I watched a clip, just now
Showing mothers and fathers scurrying
Tightly holding their terrified children's hands
Trying to take them to school.
Men in bannered white regalia
Marching – Marching!
Banging drums; whistling and shouting
Marching. Righteous soldiers
Trampling over the crying little ones
Throwing punches and stones; spitting
At the mums and dads and their children
Marching...!

The Café Down the Road on Kelham Island

It's always buzzing and humming when I walk by
Around lunchtime and sometimes tea…
It is mostly busy with students from the two universities
And professional people.
Its seats and tables are rustic – high, rectangular
Oak like at a Bavarian;
Some are low – mostly those by the wall
Holding newspapers and magazines
And those in the far window,
Through which, one can see the trees
Shedding their precious leaves
Gently swaying and dancing in the tired wind.
The window close to my writing hand
Extends the length of the café,
With stacked cans in rows of pyramids, on several shelves.
Across the road, the new eco-energy efficient flats are almost complete
They resemble a dark rich elongated wedding cake –
Shaped like steps ascending and descending the murky sky
Covered in a stainless icing.
People go by some hurrying with opened umbrellas;
One man taking great strides
Others rushing holding their shoulder bags,
Heads bowed and determined in a rejuvenating landscape.

There is only one picture on the wall – the face of a musician;
A large poster harking back to late 60s early seventies pop art.
The nose, unseeing eyes and mouth areas are black
The rest white – like one of Marc Bolan, I saw when I was at school,
And the 'Free Angela Davis and all Political Prisoners' posters
At the time of Gil Scott Heron's 'Winter in America.'
As it's almost here on this island – from which the Pilgrims sailed…
"Ain't nobody fighting 'cause nobody knows what to save."
On the stereo, Jamaica seeps through heavy bass and drums – Sly and Robbie
When someone comes in or leaves, the passing cars sound like a thousand people
Suddenly insisting a person to shush at a classical concert…

I sit drinking camomile tea and eating croissants without butter or jam,
Brought on a small enamel plate; similar to a polio medical dish containing
Sugared tablets and a prickly thing that determined who should have the jab.
Funny, the irony of patient and loyal time – no syringe but things the body needs.
Opposite – her hair is the colour of harvested wheat, in a ponytail, resting on the nape of her neck, against a spotted blouse that switches patterns when she moves…
Each crease pressed smooth, when she bends forward,
To sip her drink or to take a bite from her piece of walnut cake on another enamel plate.
It's getting busy. People snared by the aroma of ground coffee traipse in…

The café shines yellow and bright,
Like a star – a mirror reflecting against the darkening day.
Those ordering or moving around
Are like spectres, reflected ghosts silhouetting…
Floating on a black carpet shrouding their legs
More and more as the night rush in,
Like some secret prompting the voices to hush –
Whisper as if the night means something conspiratorial
Something different. Something sacred…
Apart from two voices penetrating inviting all to know they eat healthily.
They recognise Crane Brinton's second and fourth conditions
They are loud with acquired formal accents,
"Are revolutions born of hope…?"
Talking over the cakes stacked on the counter
Uncovered and unprotected from their falling words.
Everyone pretends not to be listening
They are 'stardust and golden…'
Pretty like the vegetables especially
The aubergines, chillies, carrots, pumpkins
And the remembrance poppies in the box by the door.

An Inch Apart

We
Sit…
An inch
Apart
Our bodies barely touching.

Our fingers meet
Momentarily,
As we pass a magazine or the TV control.

Our voices
Are the movements of fencers,
Oil on water,
The same poles of two magnets trying to make contact.

When I wake
You go to sleep.
When I go to sleep, you wake.
As I say hello
You say goodbye
And when I say goodbye
You say…

Sometimes I'd sit and watch the rain falling
Washing away the settled dust.
Reviving the withered plants,
Infecting life into the dying soil.

I'd watch the drops rippling...
Finding their way to the edges
Of each muddy pool;
And I'd think how obvious we seem to be falling apart
Like well-worn jeans, like a null hypothesis.
Our bodies desensitised, anaesthetised, tense, latent...
Our minds unoccupied, dissimilar, empty of who we were
Of where we are going. Long forgotten where we've been;
Two emotional minefields, a laceration of consciousness.

We talk in nods, polite grunts and formal gestures.
Our familiar modes exchanged for a more elaborate code...
Like strangers, oblivious of the other
We sit an inch apart
Lifeless... the living dead. Blind...

Caliban

Pray for me, my mother,
Even though I know
There is nothing beyond the sky…
Only the stars
Like those that twinkled in your holy eyes.

Light a candle for me, my mother
To guide my path,
To give me good grace,
To show the essence of my worth.

I'm their carnivalesque;
A thing to know when they're drunk
I'm no bad thing to behold in the dead of night.

Funny, they dance to my music,
They know the words to our sweet, sweet songs.
But they are ignorant and blind they don't really see me
Only when they are alone.

Sing a hymn for me, mother
A psalm of David,
A song to bring their cruel
Stubborn walls tumbling to the ground.

Sing a song for me,
My darling mother…
A song of joy
A song of love
Like the love, I feel for you.

Halfway

Lights hit the street
Bouncing off the wet tarmac
From the drizzling rain.
The wheels of cars and bikes ripple,
Snake to the edges of muddy puddles
Reflecting the colours of tail lights –
Advertisements and logos on the sides of the trams,
Dancing oranges and blues
Like when I think of you tonight;
When I'll meet you coming from Halfway.
Would you wear what you do, when you make your promises?
Will the stark, dark night shine its light on you?
Showing your pulsating veins and your rich sinew?
The lights spill gently and hard
On the rain-swept street,
Leading to stop and wait
All the way from Halfway
And me at Cathedral,
Listening to the clock chime seven
Fascinated that the hands of time
Are not affected by the pounding rain,
Lashing God's angels standing on plinths of stone;
Hovering high above on leaded stained glass,
Like you floating to me on tracks of steel
Synonymous with these streets beneath my soaked feet
Tapping impatiently on the wet concrete platform
The same as my pregnant heart eagerly waiting for you
From Halfway...

The Interview

She sits, staring at my moving lips
Guessing, I think,
The thoughts in my eyes,
Surveying me as I nervously play with my fingertips.

Crossed legged and hunched;
Her right hand cupping her chin
Her left hand beating an inaudible rhythm on her knee...

Her eyes sparkling like diamonds,
Move with my every sway
Darting looks at my unsure postures
And my agitated ease.

When I make a joke,
Her pupils dilate,
Like a focusing camera.
Her forehead acknowledging her widening smile
Furrow knowingly.

She asks me questions,
In a soft caressing tone
Like a mother soothes a child to sleep.

My answers come unreluctantly,
Revealing more than I had in mind...
Saying the things, I'd rehearsed not to say
Exposing more of me than mere words.

She stands for me to go,
Unwinding like a meandering river,
Her embrace enfolds me, kissing me on both cheeks
At the same time disconnecting me like a plug,
Leaving me in a haze of perfume and warm thank-yous.

As she strides across the room
She takes a last backward glance,
Eyeing me with a wry smile
Breathing goodbye.

This Coat

This coat, you've given me,
Has no outlets for my arms,
No vents at the front nor at the back.
When I move it wraps me,
Like, cling film containing packaged meat.
The strings at the neck strangle;
Making it impossible to breathe
I cannot look north, south, east or west…
Why did you choose it in a faded colour?

Orb

"I feel it
Twisting, breathing
This stone!
Its rushing speed
Slowly revolving.
It's strange, but I know
I've been here predynastic
Before the beginning…!
Longer than you know
Or can imagine.
I know,
Call it what you want,
That I'm closer to it
Than mere words can convey
More than you can understand or know
More than I can make you know!

It knows,
In its quiet solitude,
Its creations and manifestations
It knows its first born…
Its order of things
Most essentially,
It knows that I know
It's existence before Horus
It knows I was there
When Ma'at came to be.

I can't explain
But I've been here a long, long time.
I'm linked to this orb; its whispers and sighs
Its muted voice… its sorrows
Its mountains,
Its red dust road… its all giving river,
Like hot desert sand
Imbedded in the sinew of me
The purrs and raptures of my soul.
I hear its cries
I'm attuned to its groans
Its ecstasy and its distress
It's tiredness…
Its betrayal of me!"

Bumped into Jesus

I bumped into Jesus yesterday
In the Cloud9 café.
Before I uttered a word
He said,
"I forgive you
Forgive you for what you're about to say
Forgive you for saying it anyway."

"Will there come a day?" I asked,
"Come a day when you walk among us?
Not just sharing your bread and wine with me here
But...
When you step out of your shroud
Clouding our thoughts of what you're supposed to be?
To judge our actions for destruction to all...
Our greed of one for you ninety-nine for me
Our curse on humanity?"

He looked at me,
A smile spread across his face
Up to his furrowed brow.
Wiping a crumb from the side of his mouth
With the cuff of his sleeve –
"Those words I'm supposed to have said
Are not mine. I never said them...
Sure, I do endorse love, peace and helping each other
But those words are yours – Man's
Thought of when you were most likely sitting at home

Feeling pleased and smug with yourself
Shut far away from the wrongs you do
It's just a pity you cannot enact them
Blinkered in your spite and hunger
For what the other has!"

Then he laughed
Really laughed, almost choking
Coughing and spluttering his wine down his chin
Crazily, like a maniac.
"When will you learn…? Playing with things that burn,
Then saying you do them in my name; for Me?
Aye?
Aye?
Christ!" He screamed
When he finally caught his breath and composed himself.
"You lot
You lot…!
You really take the biscuit."

Skinned Knuckles

I rushed to her as soon as I heard,
Descending the stairs in twos and threes
From work
Every light seemed permanently on red
Especially my green;
The summer sky suddenly cloaked, in hues of grey,
Hastened to veil all that was true

She was lying on a bed on a busy ward,
Surrounded by people talking all at once –
Trying to prepare me.
She sighed tiredly and fumbled for my hand,
When I sat on the edge of the bed by her side;
The skin stretched tightly across her skinned knuckles.
She strained to give me one of her special smiles
That only seemed to dim the stars in her beautiful eyes
Her breathing, already travelled a distance unknown,
Reluctantly returned as if to pay me one last visit
As if to say…

I tried to caress her
But a voice said no
No, it's best not to!
Then I cried – my whole inside raw…
Tears flowing when she whispered,
"Don't be sad my beautiful nightingale
This is not goodbye, my nightingale…

I love you. Love you!"
Whilst attempting to wipe away the tears
Upon my despondent cheeks,
Her eyes heavy with pain,
"This is not the end, please don't cry!"
Then she fought –
Fought to embrace me, one last time
Her weak trembling kiss, her goodbye.

Ideo Lou Gee

Words coming from you don't mean anything.
They fall from your mouth, without a thought,
Effortlessly,
Aiming to maim
Devoid of reasons –
Unintentional at the same time intentional

I think if you weren't a person,
You would be a sword, a knife...
An implement made of cold steel
Forged by a Smith lovingly
To withstand any ferocity,
To penetrate with the minimum of thrust;
To inflict the maximum pain

Barren is your mind,
In its absence of emotions;
Love, hate, happiness, sadness
Consideration, compassion – reason.
I reach out to you on bended knees
And outstretched arms.
My body lying at your feet like a dog prostrated
A supplicant.

You walk never looking down
Never hearing a sound…
Consumed in your world of self-satisfaction and ignorance
Your ideas and beliefs.
If I promise to say not a word
If I promise to shed not a tear
If I promise to give all that you want of me…
Would that bend you like a forgiving saint?
Would you change the way you are?

Kings and Generals, Clergies and Missionaries

The call echoes
Through the valleys, the corridors
And the polished halls.
I see streamers flying across the sky
And fireworks exploding into showers,
Flowering the darkness...
But I am disillusioned by the words
Frightened by the meaning of them all.

I am not bound to follow
Anything that's about to fall
Off a steep precipice,
Because of contradictions and convictions
Bundled up in disguised intent and allegorical vitriol.

Kings and Generals, Clergies and Missionaries
Spew the meaning of being.
Pander the notion of togetherness,
With God and Christ going before they lead into war
The cause unimportant,
As long as they stay as they are.

The funeral cars draped in emblems over coffins
Containing the seeds born through agony,
Cut down in territories deemed to be ordained by God;
Demarcated by Kings and Generals, Clergies and Missionaries.

Oh, their speeches sparkle like the wine
Denied to us to keep its price high…
Their status boosted by the lies
We swallow in our pathetic inability to ask why

And as they reside in palaces and temples –
The keepers of our invisible psyche,
Far away from the scythes,
Far away from the tools of their wanton actions and lies
Far away from death's cries,
The carnage is nailed down in coffins
Or stacked high on funeral pyres…
The empty rhetoric of condolence
Accompanied by trumpet sounds and bugle calls,
Processions and pageantries
In the name of historical inheritance,
National heritage and patriotism,
Through greatness sang upon millions of lips.

Like vultures, they perch,
Stuffed full with the spoils of their victories
Elated in their deeds,
Eloquence and speeches of democracy;
Celebratory in their status
Of Kings and Generals, Clergies and Missionaries

Security

I hear the thoughts going around my head
Feel the vibration pumping the adrenaline
I am super ferocious, supercharged super frustrated

I hear the encouraged yes in my mind
But the prevailing no echoes through the bastion of my life,
As I climb each foothold secured Ixion-like restraints tug at my jaws

I'm falling, I'm falling there seems no end
My body shatters on rocks of mockery and I told you so's.

I feel the tension around my wrist as a purgatory knot anchors me
In a liquid straitjacket, drowning my optimistic thoughts into
Pessimistic hesitation and rages of solitude and gloom.

I run feeling free, free and liberated, my whole being emancipated
In my thought songs are sung, but as I look around, I see I'm on a treadmill
My reality an improbability

My tears fall tasting like the sweat my worn self perspires
Tasting like the sea that I know can extinguish this fire.

If security weren't so secured, I swear I'd throw it away
I swear I'd dance all over it, trampling it into the dirt
For I hate the lies it tells me, and I hate myself for going back for more.

About The Author

"I've been passionate about writing since an early age, particularly poems, from when I used to have books read to me and stories told to me by my grandmother. I'd say my poems are an organic process that encompass all aspects of my life and experiences; they are my composite self and reflect my senses, in particular things I see, hear and feel. I'd say most of them are not autobiographical though in truth they are. Many are stimulated by relationships (some personal), in my life and social observations. My inspirations are many, including just about everything I've read and every piece of art I've seen. However, music is by far my greatest muse. It is the food of my soul.

As well as a writer, I'm a high school teacher and keen photographer, living and working in Sheffield. Like my photography, my poems are attempts to capture moments along my life's path."

Emerson McL.Daniel

Printed in Great Britain
by Amazon

65685504R00071